The Southern Scene

Kevin Robertson

Ian Allan
PUBLISHING

First published 2008

ISBN 978 0 7110 3339 9

Published by Ian Allan Publishing

an imprint of Ian Allan Publishing Ltd, Hersham, Surrey KT12 4RG
Printed in England by Ian Allan Printing Hersham, Surrey KT12 4RG

Code: 0810/B2

Visit the Ian Allan Publishing website at www.ianallanpublishing.com

Introduction

Two decades ago a book appeared entitled *Southern Reflections: A Collection of Photographs from the Hulton Picture Library*. The views were a revelation, as they depicted scenes from the pre-Nationalisation period taken by professional photographers at a time when most railway enthusiasts equipped with a camera restricted themselves to the conventional three-quarter view.

Here then were photographs from professional press photographers whose work graced the newspapers and glossy magazines of the time. When published at the time it was unfortunate that all too often such views were cruelly 'cropped' or else reproduced as a series of far from flattering dots on poor quality newsprint.

The impact in seeing this standard of photograph 'in the raw' was immediate and profound. The *Southern Reflections* title was destined to be just one of four similar books, each following a like theme, dealing with one of the 'Big Four' railway companies that operated virtually all of the railway network before 1948.

Hulton was one of what were several photographic archives whose records could be traced back a number of decades. *Picture Post*, Topical Press, Fox Photographs, Peter Popple and others all vied with each other to record not only contemporary and newsworthy events, but also to build up a stock collection of views which might then be used both in articles and similarly as 'fillers' should the occasion arise on a 'slow news day'.

The images themselves were invariably taken using a plate camera or with a high quality negative film, certainly in excess of the resources of most amateurs of the time. Additionally the photographers themselves had not only to be skilled in the manipulation of the various items they carried around, but also be able to spot a potential subject, this particular aspect being perhaps the key to the appeal of the collection.

A standard front end view of a locomotive might have impact, but add the staff, perhaps affixing a headboard, and the view takes on a whole new meaning. Likewise there was always the tried and trusted formula guaranteed to tug at the heartstrings of the reader — the small child against the background of the locomotive, a portrait that features on numerous occasions. Additionally the railways themselves were regularly in the public eye. This may appear a little difficult to understand nowadays but decades ago events affecting the railway were newsworthy and invariably praised, compared with the all-to critical approach today.

A newsworthy event then might see photographers descend from a variety of directions. The newspaper staff themselves, freelance individuals and the photographic agencies of the type now under discussion. Each would vie with the other for the best vantage point or the 'scoop' which also explains why in what follows there is sometimes a choice of several photographs showing the same event but from slightly different angles.

The photographers themselves had in some ways to be artists, in the same way that a good commercial photographer today will still achieve better results with limited equipment compared with the man in the street possessing the latest digital technology.

With most photograph agencies based in the capital it is understandable that the majority of views should feature the London area; the gems that have been located from elsewhere are all the more remarkable and therefore worthy of inclusion.

Moving film footage was contemporary with the photographs agencies — British Movietone News and Pathe Picture Pictorial are two of the best known moving image libraries whose work was seen at almost every cinema throughout the land.

Changing times and especially the coming of television to a mass audience meant the end, first of the cinema newsreel and then the photographic agencies. Some still exist today, but in a totally different form whilst the call for images of times past is limited. For this reason the Radio Times Hulton Picture Library is no more and now forms part of the Getty media empire. The Getty archive also encompasses the work of many of the other photographic agencies.

In 2006 I approached the Getty archive with a view to use some of its material for a new series of Southern Railway-related books. Following negotiation this was agreed, although it was perhaps a slight shock to be advised of the rates involved bearing in mind the limited interest and in consequence print run of most railway books nowadays.

The response to the material I did use was both profound and unexpected. I was delighted when Ian Allan Publishing agreed to sponsor the publication of an album of similar views, something I could not in any way have considered myself.

To have access to what was virtually an untapped archive was to be like the proverbial child in a sweet shop. As the reader can imagine it was very easy to become sidetracked, as indeed we often were, on totally unrelated photographic topics.

The practicalities of such numbers of prints and negatives must also be realised. There could well be hidden away gems which it is just not possible or practical to locate, certainly not in the terms of a human lifetime. Consequently I restricted myself to those views that were readily accessible.

Of the photographs themselves, these have been selected from several viewpoints: historical interest, photographic content and personal appeal. I hope that having a regular audience with a number of railway enthusiasts has enabled me to make a choice that will indeed be appealing.

One final thing I would mention is to record my thanks to several people without whose help none of this would have been possible. First, Peter, Nick and Nigel at Ian Allan for having faith in the idea. After all, it is not every day that someone turns up and states 'I want you to spend some money (quite a bit in fact) on my behalf'. Then, at Getty itself, Catherine, whom I am quite sure must have exceeded her job description on a number of occasions in providing advice and innumerable photo copies, as well as regularly pointing the way to the ever welcome coffee machine. Finally, to Bruce, a professional photographer himself, who knows a fine image when he sees one.

Kevin Robertson
Hampshire 2008

Press photography only really got going in the 1920s. Before this time, the broadsheet style newspapers entertained their readership with column after column of text leavened with only the occasional engraving. Thus views dating from World War I period or earlier are hard to find. This view of a South Eastern & Chatham Railway coach containing a saloon at Charing Cross station is entitled 'First-class Equipment'. The upholstered lower half of the open door is typical of First Class accommodation of the time. The carriage has brackets for roof boards.

Above: The overhead electrification introduced by the London Brighton & South Coast Railway changed markedly the appearance of the railway through Clapham Junction. A veritable forest of wires can be seen here at the eastern end of Britain's busiest junction station, in the years before the Southern Railway opted for the third rail electrification pioneered by the London & South Western Railway. Today the semaphore signals, as well as the catenary, are long gone, although of course overhead electrification has spread over much of the rest of the railway system.

Below: Tests involving an 'autocoupler', at lancing in the early days of the Southern Railway, the assembled gathering including some female spectators. The presence of the latter would appear to be slightly unusual assuming them to be official visitors in what was then a very much male dominated industry. The difficulty with the provision of any type of automatic coupling at this time, whether successful or not, was persuading the railway companies to adopt it.

Top left: This photograph, taken on 1 August 1913, shows a group of schoolboys using an early weighing machine at Waterloo station. The hoarding behind the weighing machine looks to be temporary, and implies rebuilding work in progress. The station was rebuilt to its modern form in the last years of the LSWR, and underwent further major transformation in the 1990s when the Eurostar terminal was constructed on the site of the Windsor Lines platforms.

Left: Trackwork underway at Charing Cross station. The station received a new roof in 1907 — the building material stacked on the platform may well be associated with the new roof, rather than the permanent way activity. The men appear to be working without the protection of a lookout, but he could, of course, be out of view of the camera.

Above: Service personnel are seen queuing at Victoria station during World War 1, to change their foreign currency back into sterling (or vice versa). An officer is taking his place in the queue with the NCOs.

Above: The notes accompanying this print state that it is of Major Richardson and his bloodhounds 'on their way to the front'. The location was not recorded, but is likely to have been one of the London termini. The dog carries Red Cross insignia — 'bloodhounds' were of great use in searching out injured men in the battlefield.

Top right: Ascot in 1908, with porters busy unloading goods for a race meeting. The presence of a policeman may be pure coincidence, or perhaps the boxes contained items of great value.

Right: Swanwick station in Hampshire, on the line from St Denys to Fareham. At the time this photograph was taken, the station had been open for just over 20 years and the line had not long been widened to double track. The railway remains open here as part of the electrified route between Southampton and Portsmouth.

Left: Although bearing the identity 'S&D No 23', this locomotive was never actually delivered to the Somerset & Dorset Joint Railway. It was one of a batch of six such engines with 17in by 22in cylinders, 5ft driving wheels and a grate area of 17sq ft, which were built by Vulcan Foundry for the S&D, being completed in July 1866. Only two of the six, Nos 19 and 20, were delivered to the S&D owing to financial difficulties. Instead, the other four were sold to the Alsace Lorraine Railways in France. An unlikely picture for a newspaper photograph library, this view was taken at the Vulcan works. The pair that were delivered to the S&D were renumbered Nos 15 and 16, and remained in service until 1913/4.

Below left: A view of Ashey on the Isle of Wight taken in October 1923. A racecourse was nearby, which generated traffic for this stop on the line between Newport and Ryde. Today the line through here is part of the Isle of Wight Steam Railway.

Below: Ashey station, showing the presence of what appears to be the stock of a special train, which was likely to have been run in connection with the nearby racecourse. Slotted post signals, as seen here, were already rather old-fashioned by the 1920s, although the last in use on BR survived at Haxby in North Yorkshire until the 1980s.

Left: The marshalling yard at Feltham, Middlesex, was brought into use in stages between December 1917 and April 1922. Taken somewhere between these two dates, this view shows temporary buffers at the then limit of the yard. The three brake vans are of Panter's design and illustrate a type which survived for many years. Termed 'Road Vans', some of these LSWR vehicles were still active on the Isle of Wight railways in the 1960s.

Below: The South Eastern side of Victoria station. The LBSCR half of the station, is out of sight to the right of the photograph. The majority of passengers using Victoria were of course, heading to destinations in Kent and Sussex, but both the SE&CR and LBSCR could not resist giving prominence on the exterior to the more exotic destinations reached from the Channel ports, to which the station was the gateway.

Right: LSWR passenger brake van No 4729 is seen at an unknown location being loaded with strawberries. There was considerable traffic in soft fruit from Hampshire and the stations at Swanwick and Botley are likely locations for this undated picture.

Left: During World War 1, a number of large ambulance trains were created by the railway companies for use on the other side of the Channel. This is US Ambulance Train No 62, which was formed in April 1918. Its 16 bogie vehicles could accommodate up to 620 persons, made up of patients, medical staff and orderlies, plus train crew. It is seen at Eastleigh.

Bottom left: This view is described as being the dining interior of a South Western Railway ambulance train at Eastleigh in May 1918. This would appear to be an area of the train intended for Officers. The potted plant looks a little vulnerable to the effects of a rough shunt.

Below: Unknown facilities, although possibly Kitchen Car D1/603 from the 1918 ambulance train set set and recorded in May 1918. Beyond the partition at the end of the kitchen area was a compartment having three beds, a pantry, and linen store. The whole train was of course corridor connected, the door to which is just visible to the right of the partition. Behind the camera was a seating area for 'Sick Officers' again accessed by a side corridor.

Top left: Concluding this small sequence of contemporary Ambulance trains is this view, again reported as May 1918, but clearly now at Waterloo. This would appear to be Set No 62 with the official caption referring to a 'Red Cross Train'. This may then have been the occasion of an official inspection of the facilities. Conversions of vehicles for medical use had been taking place, on the LSWR at least, since 1900.

Left: The 1919 railway strike was an opportunity to record working in what were unusual circumstances. Here 'London's milk supply is arriving at Waterloo' sometime between 27 September and 5 October 1919. Contingency plans ensured that on the Sunday 28 September, the line was used solely for the movement of milk and foodstuffs destined for London. The strike had come about due to the Government wishing to double the men's wages in lieu of the War-Wage system which had up to that time ensured staff wages rose in line with inflation. Despite the potential doubling of wages the men would have been considerably worse off and the Government did in fact concede. Even so and not withstanding an increase in establishment from 24,000 to 31,000 staff between 1913 and 1921, the annual wage bill for the LSWR rose from £2 million to £6 million over the same period.

Above: Against a wonderful background of various horse-drawn wagons themselves mounted on flat trucks, the Australian Cricket team poses for the camera upon arrival in England — presumably there were more of them somewhere? The view is both undated and without a location being stated, although it may be reasonable to assume it was probably taken at Southampton. Decades later it was fortunate indeed the camera recorded the background — the reason of course for selecting the view for inclusion now. It is perhaps a little surprising that such a background was in fact used. Was this a 'rushed shot'?

Left: 'T9' class 4-4-0 No 304 is seen at Waterloo in March 1921, while a wagon belonging to Stephenson Clarke displays its ownership details.

Bottom left: Bishop Heard is photographed at Waterloo with his niece Miss Valerie Caldwell on 18 August 1937. The bishop was making his way to Southampton to board the *Queen Mary* on his return to New York after a conference. In an example of colour discrimination, the Bishop had been refused accommodation in Edinburgh on account of his race.

Below: On 1 June 1937, Derby racer Bambino arrives at Epsom station by special train a day before the big race, (The race was subsequently won by Mid Day Sun.)

Below: Some of the views in the Getty collection have no details as to why they were taken, including this picture. Taken at Brighton, it depicts a cross-country train, whose journey might well taken 6-8hr.

Bottom: The booking hall at Victoria (Eastern side), after rebuilding. The booking hall had been badly damaged in wartime and opened in its rebuilt form on 5 May 1951. Three years after Nationalisation, the by-laws posters were still bearing the 'Southern Railway' heading. The words accompanying this photograph referred to the facility's central heating and fluorescent lighting. The then-fashionable duffle coat suggests that this day in May was not particularly warm.

Right: The Eastern concourse at Victoria is uncharacteristically deserted during a strike in October 1962. Where thousands of passengers would normally be bustling to and fro, a lone policeman surveys the station.

Left: This view of the observation car of the 'Devon Belle' captures some of the style with which the Southern Railway launched the train in 1947. The coach, which in latter years would be transferred to the West Highland line in Scotland, is crossing Barnstaple bridge.

Right: The Getty archive contains a series of views entitled 'The Life of a London Station', of which this photograph, taken at Victoria, is one. The information on the back of the file print states that the station handled nearly 1,000 trains carrying 123,000 passengers daily. Pictured is a man and his dog collecting for charity. The charity involved is not identified. Readers may remember the various collecting dogs that stood stuffed and mounted on various station concourses. The collecting tins they carried were made of aluminium, with a polished brass plate, secured in place with a leather strap. The last of these dogs was at Wimbledon station in the latter years of Network SouthEast. One of the collecting tins is known to have sold for several hundred pounds at auction in 2007.

Below: 'Schools' class 4-4-0 No 903 *Charterhouse* heads away from London Bridge with what may well be a Hastings line train, the very service for which the class was intended. Pictures such as this were regularly supplied by the railways to the newspapers, in an era when the railways seem to have had a higher news value than today.

New facilities for left luggage at Victoria, shown here on 1 February 1954, the day the new lockers were brought into use. Similar installations were shortly to be provided at Brighton and Eastbourne. The lockers were 18in high, 16¾in wide and 2ft 5in deep. Concerns about terrorism or other inappropriate use of luggage lockers were a world away in 1954.

Above: Rebuilding work in progress at Exmouth. The work involved both the extension of the platforms as well as, out of sight, a new main station building. The investment by the Southern Railway at this time both here and at other West Country destinations would certainly be recuperated in later years, the Devon and Cornwall resorts popular for travellers arriving by train for almost the next 40 years.

Below: The notes on the rear of this file print state that this is Southampton in 1952. The Pullman cars are awaiting passengers disembarking from the liner *Queen Elizabeth*, which after a varied career, including service as a troop ship during World War 2, sank in Hong Kong Harbour in 1972 following on-board fires during conversion to a floating university. Customs checks on baggage appear to be taking place at the tables on the right, with as yet only a few passengers starting to board the train.

Above: Initiative being displayed. This is one of several views in the Getty collection, where staff with 'that little bit extra' were recognised. Here at Tooting, the booking clerk was particularly adept at producing neat notices.

Right: This print was entitled 'Speeding up the Laggards on the Southern Railway' — at Wimbledon in this case. Here it was reported that a Klaxon device had been installed to be used by porters to encourage passengers, by making it clear via a series of blasts, that a train was ready to start. The equipment, photographed on 5 December 1935, was operated by a push-button and was also evidently intended to advise passengers that a train was ready to stop.

Left: The lady station master at Whippingham, on the Isle of Wight was photographed in September 1908, unfortunately her name was not recorded. A lady station master was rare, but by no means unique; it is possible that the photographer was on the Isle of Wight to record some other event at the time. Whippingham, on the Newport-Ryde route, had opened as a stopping place in 1875 and being the nearest railway station to the Royal residence Osborne House, it was hoped that it might be of use to Queen Victoria, although in the event, it is not believed ever to have been used by royalty. A passing loop was provided here in 1912, but this was taken out of use and the station closed in 1953, 13 years before the railway through the station was closed.

Right: The interior of a compartment of the new stock introduced at the time of the electrification to Brighton in the early 1930s. The set type is not reported. The style and fittings seen here remained little changed for many years — the days of bland plastic, aluminium and Formica were still some way distant.

Below: At a time when the building of a by-pass was a noteworthy event, the cameraman from Fox Photos recorded work in progress on the new 400-ton bridge that was shortly to be manoeuvred into place to carry the railway across the new Guildford-Milford road. The locomotive is an 'N' class 2-6-0 and at this date, 27 April 1934, had still to receive smoke deflectors.

Below: The Easter exodus at Waterloo, sometime before 1923. The curvature of the main office block can just be determined, as can the concourse access to the Underground. Aside from the fashions, the main point of interest is the old Bodmin & Wadebridge Railway coach, which reposed here for many years. During wartime, this historic vehicle was moved for safe storage amongst the arches under the station. It now has a permanent home as part of the National Collection at York.

Right: A photograph taken at Baynards in West Sussex on 14 September 1962. In 11 years based at the country station, signalman Geoff Bardfield had transformed the station into a blaze of colour, which attracted as many visitors by road (!) as by rail. The file notes read 'Mr Bardfield, 45, has more than 240 varieties of Dhalia growing at the station and more at a local nursery — and in the greenhouse at the station, he tends some 1,000 plants each year.'

Right: This waiting room, pictured at Waterloo on 14 January 1936 might fairly be described as 'austere yet functional'. According to the caption on the back of this Fox Photos print it was 'A super new waiting room …[where] passengers need no longer grumble about the cold.' Attention was drawn to the 'up to date' lighting and 'sun trip' windows.

Left: Whitsun holiday crowds at Waterloo. This photograph is undated, but appears to be from the late 1920s or early 1930s. At least one member of railway staff, possibly a guard, is weaving his way through the throng, whilst in the foreground the other man with a railway-type cap could well be an inspector. Two other porters are visible in the background, as well as a policeman.

Below: South African athletes, who had taken part in the Empire Games, make the first part of their journey home, at Waterloo on 17 August 1934. The semaphore signals at Waterloo would be gone in a couple of years, when the new power signalbox and associated colour light signalling would be inaugurated.

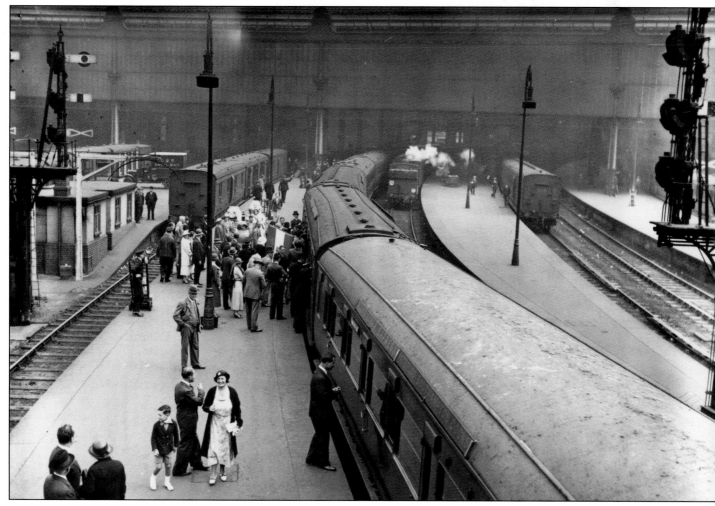

Above: One of the Life of a London Station series of views, this 11 February 1939-dated picture shows the moments after the departure of the boat train for Southampton. As the note on the back of the print puts it, 'The boat train has left, now the porters carry away the notices'.

Top right: In a Pullman car, the subjects of this Life of a London Station view 'settle down to read their comics before the journey commences.'

Right: Beneath the platforms and on the way to the subway, a selection of posters at Waterloo dated 1916. Although World War 1 was by then two years old, 'Steamship Routes to the Continent' were still being advertised. The poster announcing the commencement of electric trains on the Shepperton line from 30 January 1916 is of particular interest.

Top left: A special train for Sir Malcolm Campbell arrives at Waterloo in the first half of the 1930s. Sir Malcolm had set, and then broken, the world land speed record several times in the late 1920s and early 1930s, at Daytona Flats in the United States of America. Another photographer can be seen on the platform to the right.

Left: The country end of Waterloo station is seen from the signalbox during the strike of October 1962. Some trains appear to be running, but the place looks pretty quiet compared to the normal bustle.

Above: The final month of peace before war. This was the scene at Waterloo on Thursday 3 August 1939 and a few days before the Bank Holiday. (The August Bank Holiday was always the first Monday of August until quite recent years.) The view is obviously of the luggage of the holidaymakers but worth mentioning is that it was not always railway porters who were occupied in such roles as certainly on summer Saturday afternoons, the office clerks could earn overtime, as well as a sizeable proportion of tips, assisting at the main line termini. At the time tips were designated tax-free and these alone could amount to more than the normal week's wages. Seen here on 15 March 1935 with a new use for the manufacture and filling of bottles with pickles and sauces.

Left: A busy scene inside Bricklayers Arms Goods Depot on 15 March 1932. Pilfering from goods depots was a constant problem for the railways, with every kind of commodity being delivered and forwarded. It was said that almost anything could be 'ordered' from crooked workers at the large goods depots and at one site the situation became so bad that not only were the railway police called in, but the local constabulary were also engaged to 'watch the watchers'.

Above: Security was in evidence at Bricklayers Arms Goods Depot on 15 March 1932 when a number of art treasures were despatched by container on their way home. The packing of the container had taken 10 days before it was delivered to Bricklayers Arms.

Below: Holiday time at Littlehampton in West Sussex, August 1950. Vast numbers of trippers were carried to coastal stations such as this. Today Littlehampton remains a popular station, although the lines to its harbour wharf have been taken up. A modern station building has replaced the facilities extant in 1950.

Left: A *Picture Post* Life of a London Station view of passengers enjoying the then latest Maunsell coaching stock.

Below: The holiday rush at Waterloo, 30 July 1960. Save for the first few destinations on each board, almost all the places mentioned are no longer served by rail. There could be a long wait for those who had not reserved their seats.

Right: The Western side of Victoria station in the 1930s. Overshadowed by the then new Imperial Airways building, an 'H' class 0-4-4T stands with a works train. The air service ran from Victoria's Platform 17 to Southampton for the Empire Flying Boat service. Later the flying boat service was transferred to Poole, before returning again to Southampton. Today Victoria is host to the clock face arrivals and departures of the Gatwick Express for air travellers.

Above: Cannon Street, recorded on 19 January 1946. The station exterior looks careworn, yet it has escaped the effects of bombing of a few years earlier, something that cannot be said for the building to the right, which requires the support of timber baulks.

Top right: Waterloo on 27 July 1943. The Blitz had passed and whilst bombing raids still occurred, their intensity for the moment had lessened. The days of the Flying Bombs — the V1s and V2s — had yet to come. A war-weary public was keen to escape whenever possible and despite the exhortations of the government and the railways to traveller only when necessary and to give up ones seat to a shell, crowds were waiting for the 10.50am west of England service. There was no real escape from the war, however, as the military vehicles in the background show.

Right: Crowds throng the concourse at Waterloo on what was reported to be a cold 4 April 1947. Although the concourse remains the same in essence today, virtually all the detail in this view, such as the Light Refreshments counter, the wooden telephone kiosks and the rows of seats, doubling here as crowd control barriers, have all been replaced. The caption on the back of the print refers to the fact that the passengers were awaiting trains to Bournemouth and the Isle of Wight.

Left: A row of Belmatic ticket issuing machines at the newly rebuilt Eastern section booking hall at Victoria on 5 February 1951. There were six ticket issuing windows.

Above: The ramifications of industrial action in France, seen here at Waterloo on 7 August 1936. Striking French seamen caused the liner *Champion* to miss its call at Southampton, which in turn led to the cancellation of the boat train. The porter seems, however, to be viewing things with a wry grin. *Champion* was a 25,000-ton liner which sailed regularly between Le Harvre and New York. It was built in 1912 being mined and sunk in 1940.

Right: Described as 'A object lesson for schoolchildren', the neat copperplate hand of Mr Pat O'Brien, Head Porter at Charing Cross, seen here on 10 July 1963, 'was read by thousands'.

Above: When things go wrong. This was the Vauxhall accident of 29 August 1912. The coaches are from the 6.37am Aldershot-Waterloo train, which was stationary in the platform when it was hit at 7.15am by a light engine running tender-first from Nine Elms to Waterloo. The driver of the light engine had misread signals and collided with the stationary train at a speed of 20mph. Sadly one passenger was killed and 44 injured.

Top right: The calamity at Lewisham in 1957 was an incident that made headline news around the world. Here, instead of concentrating on the wreckage, the photographer has focused on the bystanders. The view is dated 8 December 1957.

Right: The sad aftermath at Salisbury, July 1906. Much has been written about this tragedy and yet questions still remain. Did the driver simply mistake his location or did the stability of the locomotive at speed provide the recipe for the disaster? Here the wreckage is being removed, the railwayman no doubt expressing his opinions to the policeman.

Below: Minor accidents can cause disruption and create newsworthy photo-opportunities, just as major tragedies. Delays of up to an hour and half were caused on 21 August 1958, when this lorry broke through the wall of a builders yard in Friendly Street, Deptford. Luckily the only casualty was the lorry driver and his injuries were minor, but delays in the St Johns area, where the lorry is seen being passed by a train of the then modern 'EPB' stock, were considerable.

Right: Undetected corrosion lay behind this incident at Clapham Junction in 1965. No doubt the heavy sheeting placed on the roof of Clapham 'A' signalbox to protect it during World War 2 also contributed to the failure of the gantry holding it above some of the busiest tracks in the country. The structure failed on the morning of 4 May 1965 and trains had to be turned round as far out as Surbiton, leaving Waterloo at a standstill. Here the crane has lifted one end of the structure, allowing supports to be placed underneath and which were then jacked to the required position. New steelwork was put in place and the signalbox served another 25 years.

Top: The aftermath of the smash involving three passenger trains between Cannon Street and London Bridge on 13 May 1925. Two of the trains involved are seen here, that furthest from the camera was from Erith, with an 0-4-4T in charge. Alongside are coaches from a train originating at Bromley, which had suffered a sidelong collision. A third train was affected by the obstruction of the down west line. Only one passenger was slightly injured, which taking into account the amount of broken glass was fortunate. The cause was found to be a driver missing a signal.

Above: The Raynes Park accident of 25 May 1933. The Southern Railway had the melancholy distinction for being responsible for five of the passenger deaths which occurred on the whole of the British railway network that year. The track (which was under repair) failed, derailing the train photographed. This in itself would not have been very serious but for the fact that an Up train then struck the side of the derailed coaches, causing the five deaths.

Right: Under the watchful eye of a seemingly important person, an unidentified 'King Arthur' class 4-6-0 backs out of Waterloo.

Below: The transfer of stock to the Isle of Wight. Alongside the new RMS *Queen Mary*, a six-compartment brake third is lifted ready for shipment across the Solent. A Class O2 locomotive can also be seen ready for shipment. The Isle of Wight system delighted enthusiasts by continuing to run a large number of old four-wheel coaches into the Grouping years, but other passengers no doubt welcomed this newer rolling stock, some of which was displaced by electrification of the suburban routes out of London, with open arms.

Right: A 121ft length of timber has been loaded on to no less than eight wagons at Nine Elms Goods depot. Intended for use as a ships mast, this was said to be the longest indivisible load carried by the railway. The date is not certain, but is believed to be 25 September 1923.

Bottom right: A container of fruit from Covent Garden Market is delivered to Battersea Goods Depot for transit to Paris. The renowned market's replacement, New Covent Garden, stands on the site of the former Nine Elms steam locomotive depot.

Left: This was the headboard attached to a 'Lord Nelson' 4-6-0 which was to haul Princess Elizabeth and Prince Philip from London on the first leg of their honeymoon to Romsey in Hampshire, from whence they would stay at the Broadlands home of Count Louis Mountbatten. By 1947, when the wedding took place, the 'Lord Nelsons' were no longer the most modern of the Southern Railway's express locomotives, their place having been taken by the Pacifics of Chief Mechanical Engineer O. V. S. Bulleid. Perhaps, though, a 'Nelson' was considered more reliable.

Above: Clapham Junction during the ASLEF strike of 1955. The view (from Clapham 'A' signalbox) is similar to that later captured by the artist Terence Cuneo, although his painting is full of trains rather than the groups of men here taking the opportunity to catch up on maintenance.

Right: This print is captioned 'Big Railway Tunnel Job Completed. Polhill Tunnel to reopen tomorrow'. The story reads: 'One of the most interesting and difficult pieces of railway track relaying will come to an end tonight when Polhill Tunnel, the second longest tunnel on the Southern Region will reopen ahead of time and after a closure of three weeks. The first train due, the 3.45am newspaper service from London Bridge to Hastings and Dover. So new have been the methods employed with special track laying equipment, that Chief Engineers from all the other regions have visited the tunnel to witness the work in progress, and technical descriptions are being sent to all parts of the world. The normal length of time for a job of this nature would have been 26 weekends with speed restrictions in operation for the whole of the time, but by diverting trains and closing the tunnel completely and with highly trained gangs the whole job was completed in three weeks.' The tunnel entrance near to Knockholt is pictured on 21 March 1948.

Left: This photograph of signal repeaters in a signalbox believed to be that at Cannon Street is part of the Life of a London Station series.

Below: Inside Waterloo power signalbox. At 11.00am, the 'Atlantic Coast Express' will be departing shortly. The clipboards will contain details of any special or out of course workings.

Left: A three-position upper quadrant signal at London Bridge. A 'King Arthur' 4-6-0, No 799 *Sir Ironside* stands in the background, its smokebox obscured by steam.

Above: Colour light signals, believed to be outside Victoria, receive maintenance.

Right: The 1935 picture shows Mrs Cordery, a railwayman's wife, whose house was between the Reading and Aldershot lines at Ascot. No doubt she was used to noise and vibration, but the smoke from passing trains must have been galling on wash days. In January 1939 the electrification of passenger services past her house must have been a godsend, but steam would continue on goods trains for many more years.

Left: A striking view of the ventilation shafts to the tunnel under Shakepseare Cliff, Dover, with smoke rising . The notes with this print refer to the Southern Railway's attempt in 1937 to obtain parliamentary powers for a new line in tunnel to replace the line running largely at the foot of the cliffs between Folkestone and Dover. If the new line had been built it would have involved no less than four and a half miles of tunnel. The intention was to reduce the risk to services from landslides and coastal erosion, which have plagued the route for many years. In the event the new alignment was never built. World War 2 interrupted its planning and the scheme was not resurrected. Although the scheme would have been very costly, its abandonment is perhaps surprising given that a major slip interrupted the route in 1939.

Below: In 1933 a bitter dispute over a level crossing at Dungeness erupted between the Southern Railway and Lydd Town Council. For a while there was no access to Dungeness from Lydd over the crossing and a police presence was required to straighten things out. The reasons for the dispute are not recorded, but strength of feeling was such that the closed gates were damaged by being forced open during the night.

Left: Towards the end at Nine Elms Goods. Here Porter William Clark uses an old bell inscribed with the initials of the LSWR to warn road users as vans are shunted across Nine Elms Lane. The notes with the print record 'The date is 21 July 1967, steam working has ceased and the TOPS computer is about to come on-stream and with it the beginning of the end for wagons and movements of this type.'

Above: A new use for an old station, well the platform and buildings at least. The location is Lewes Road, Brighton, closed on 2nd January 1933 and now with a new use for the manufacture and filling of bottles with pickles and sauces. Trains though were still passing through. 15th March 1935.

These views depict the testing of the Stowger-Hudd Automatic Train Control system at Byfleet on 7 October 1931. The system was the forerunner of the later Automatic Warning System (AWS) used by BR where magnets would either be energised or not, depending upon the speed of the train. Unlike contemporary practice on the GWR, there was no physical contact between the locomotive and the magnet. Mr Hudd, seen in the close-up view between the rails in front of the locomotive — and not wearing a hat — was keen to promote his invention, which could be used both on locomotives and multiple-units. In the event, the Southern Railway opted to invest in further colour light signalling, which it regarded as a better use of its resources. The Railway's logic was that its intensive services in the London area would cause drivers to be cancelling the warning so often that it might become an automatic reaction. The London Midland & Scottish Railway did invest in the Hudd system and installed it on the Fenchurch Street-Tilbury line where fog was a major problem. It took a major accident, in the form of the Harrow & Wealdstone crash in 1952, before progress really began to be made towards AWS installation, and even then, it was many years before the Southern Region was dealt with.

Above: Track relaying at Waterloo, 8 May 1936. Platforms 1-3 were closed for nine days while a revised arrangement of crossovers was introduced, to reduce congestion. Some 200 men were employed on the job. This photograph was taken from underneath the mechanical signalbox, which was shortly to be removed and replaced by the power signalbox.

Left: Painters on the roof of Cannon Street station, 11 March 1936. The roof ladder is supported across the framework. It would appear that climbing down was more difficult than getting up.

Below: The notes on this print describe it as the LSWR signal school at Wimbledon. The building is of typical LSWR signalbox construction, even down to the sliding windows. In later years an improved signalling school, complete with model railway and lever frames was constructed above the footbridge at Clapham Junction, only to be destroyed by fire.

Above: Thousands of jobs normally performed by men were taken up by women during World War 2, as men were needed for the military. Here Mrs Exford works a turntable, possibly at Nine Elms. It will be noted that No 850 *Lord Nelson* has its cabside window plated over.

Right: Clearing up after enemy action, 12 September 1946. At Portsmouth, a bombing raid in June 1940 caused extensive damage to Harbour station, causing several vehicles of electric multiple-unit stock to fall into the harbour. According to the caption of this print, these coaches had been salvaged by two 20-ton cranes and the placed on new bogies, before being taken away for repair. Six years' immersion in sea water do not seem to have had much effect on the carriages, which raises the question as to whether the date on the print is indeed correct. Vehicles of EMU stock in the harbour would have posed quite a serious hazard to navigation over six years!

These photographs, which were passed for use by the censor on 10 February 1941, show the fire fighting train. This contained six locomotive tenders having a total capacity of 15,000 gallons and a 20hp petrol engine powering two hoses able to deliver a 60lb/sq in jet of water for 2½hr. It was stated that 'the equipment could deal with any fire near to the tracks although there was also now the grave task of dealing with incendiary bombs that may fall on goods yards and stationary trains.'

Left: A mobile railway workshop, converted from a passenger luggage van, is being inspected at Waterloo on 29 March 1940. Several such conversions were made, each being formed into a set of vehicles, fitted with power plant, machine tools and stores, their intended use being for the British Expeditionary Force in France. None of the vans so converted ever found their way back to Southern Railway stock.

Below: A Class M7 0-4-4T receives a power wash from two lady workers on 1 October 1942. Mrs Hurst (left) was a former lift attendant, and her colleague was Mrs Walker, whose husband was a prisoner of war at the time.

Right: A typical morale-boosting view, intended to show that every one was 'doing their bit', this is Mrs Pearce (left) and Mrs Ray, with the driving wheels of a 4-6-0. The location was not recorded, but the date is given as 30 January 1943.

Right: Mrs Hilda Brown (formerly a cook) is seen receiving instruction in the mechanics of a small signalbox from District Relief Signalman P. Higham on 25 June 1943.

Far right: These lady workers are painting a railway bridge, possibly outside Waterloo station. The caption, dated 14 July 1942, remarks 'They soon acquired the sense of balance necessary to work from a plank laid across the step ladders!'

Bottom right: The first of the Bulleid Pacifics, 'Merchant Navy' No 21C1 is pictured on its inaugural run, from Eastleigh to Alresford, on 10 March 1941. The photograph was taken between Allbrook and Shawford.

Above: This appears to be the naming ceremony for No 21C5 *Canadian Pacific*. The locomotive appears to be in brand new condition although the date and location of the photograph are not given. Today, *Canadian Pacific* is the oldest of the surviving Bulleid Pacifics.

Right: A 'Lord Nelson' 4-6-0 at Waterloo on 20 January 1927. Several test runs were made to evaluate both the test equipment and the steaming efficiency of the locomotive, measured amongst other ways by taking pyrometric temperature readings. The metal observation cabin placed on the front of the locomotive is an improvement on the timber shelters which were previously used for such tests.

Left: This photograph shows a 'King Arthur' class being tested with black-out curtains. The conditions for the crew during 'sealed-in' running conditions must have resembled a sauna.

Below: A special working for Royal Ascot leaves Waterloo in June 1923. The locomotive is 'L11' 4-4-0 No 155, one of several of the class later converted to burn oil in the latter days of the Southern Railway.

Right: An unidentified Class F1 4-4-0 at Charing Cross. The former SE&CR 'F1s' dated back to 1873, although a number, such as this example, were rebuilt by Wainwright with a domed boiler. The unrebuilt examples had all been withdrawn by 1930, while a number of the rebuilt survivors saw service on LMS metals on loan during World War 2.

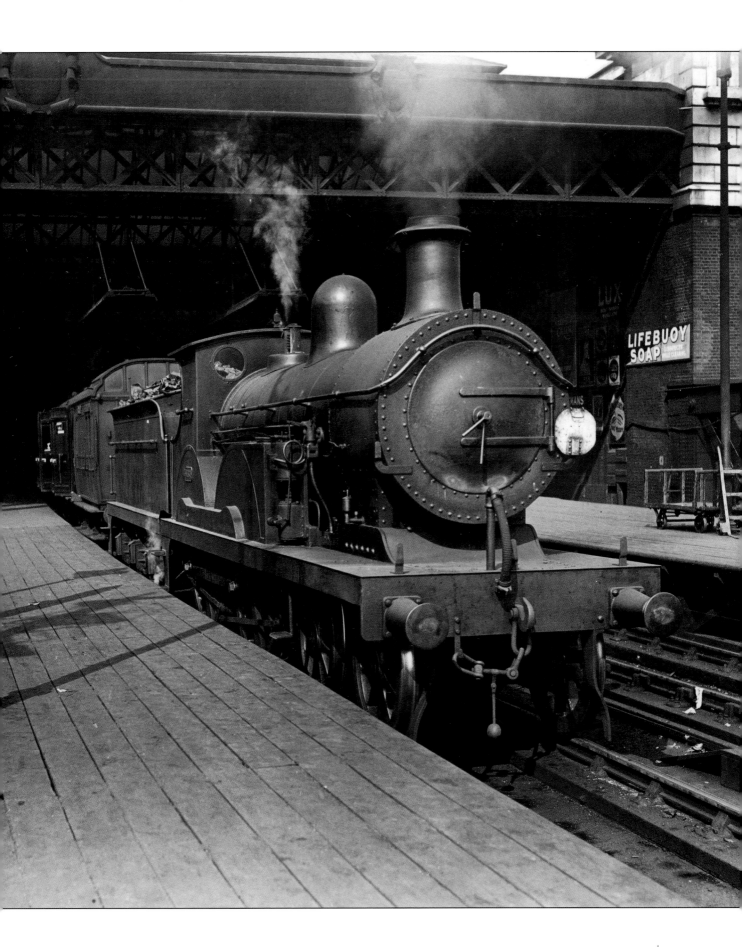

Above: A Class C 0-6-0, No 1186, at Waterloo. These were not regular locomotives at the former LSWR terminus, and the caption details on the file print, rather than explaining its appearance there, serve only to muddy the waters. A date of 1923 is given for the photograph, whereas this locomotive is known not to have received Southern Railway livery until 1925. Additionally, the notes state that the locomotive was at Waterloo in connection with the 'Continental Express'. This train, which from 1929 was renamed the 'Golden Arrow', was never associated with Waterloo, always using Victoria instead.

Left: Visitors to the Eastleigh Works Open Day in August 1950 thrill to the sight of 'Merchant Navy' No 35024 *East Asiatic Company* being lifted high above its wheels. At the time, No 35024 was just 18 months old; to the right can be seen 'Battle of Britain' class No 34090 *Sir Eustace Missenden — Southern Railway*, while a 'Q' class 0-6-0 reposes on the opposite side.

Right: At Waterloo in 1932 a group of hikers are recorded speaking to the driver of a 'T14' 4-6-0 awaiting departure. Given the steam escaping from the safety valves it might be wondered how much conversation was actually possible! All the 'T14s' were at that time based at Nine Elms shed and were used on semi-fast services to Portsmouth, Bournemouth and Salisbury.

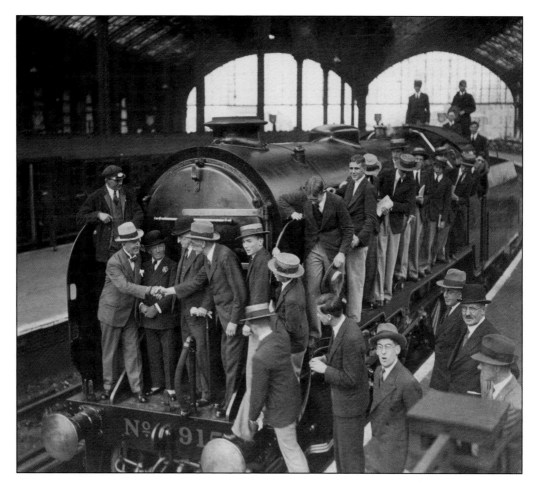

Left: Neither the date nor the location of this photograph were recorded, although the latter looks as if it could be Clapham Junction. Luckily the days of overhead wires at Clapham had passed, for the photographer must have been occupying a rather precarious position on the tender of this 'Schools' class 4-4-0. The needle on the pressure gauge indicates a good head of steam, allowing the fireman a moment to take an interest in the actions of the photographer. The coal in the tender does not appear to be of the best quality, with a lot of dust present!

Above: A new locomotive named after a local feature was always good for a few column inches and here the Southern Railway has evidently understood the publicity value of its new 'Schools' class locomotive No 915 *Brighton*. The engine is at Brighton station on 10 October 1933, being inspected by the collegers, the Mayor and other dignitaries. Interestingly, the news report refers to the locomotive as 'Brighton College', rather than its more succinct correct name.

Below: On 21 October 1933 'Lord Nelson' No 860 *Lord Hawke* is seen at Portsmouth together with a rake of seven of the latest coaches. It appears to be the locomotive rather than its train which are attracting the interest of the Lord Mayor, Lady Mayoress and other officials.

Right: The effects of priming in the form of streaks down the side of the firebox are evident to this passenger viewing 'King Arthur' No 770 *Sir Prianius* at Victoria in February 1939. Legend has it that at the time of King Arthur's supposed conquest of Rome, Sir Gawain located Prianius there, who was then baptised and knighted.

Left: Health & safety rules today would not permit the close acquaintance with the front end of a Bulleid 'Battle of Britain' class that was enjoyed by these children at the Eastleigh Open Day of 14 August 1958.

Below: A supposed 'tug of war' between two 'A12s' and 4-6-0 No 453 *King Arthur* is depicted outside Eastleigh Works on an unknown date. According to the report which accompanies the photograph, 'the other two put up a good fight before being beaten by the new Pacific [sic]'.

Right: 'Cleans Railway Engines in record Time' is the heading that accompanied this illustration and related news item dated 23 May 1946. At a time of labour difficulties and rising costs, the report reads: 'With the aid of a small instrument known as "Jenny", Britain's railway engines will soon be cleaner, brighter, and a locomotive which previously took a week to clean, can now be made to look almost like new in seven hours. "Jenny" is a small paraffin driven engine, which sprays steam mixed with a mild acid at a pressure of 150 pounds per square inch. Oil and dirt dissolve like magic, and the paint assumed a new brightness. "Jenny" enables any fault to be detected quickly, and some parts of the underneath of the engine can be cleaned in 10 minutes, compared with 10 hours by hand.'

Right: These boys are having the outside motion of 'Lord Nelson' No 860 explained to them.

Left: Location unknown, although the caption tells us exactly the circumstances and date, 20 February 1943. 'Herbert Lunn, a Southern Railway main line driver, is very proud of his allotment, which is situated in a Goods Yard. He has been looking after it since 1914 and has supplied his own family with fresh vegetables for nearly 30 years.'

Below: 'Wimbledon's Wonderful Week', sometime we know between 1927 and 1935 but unfortunately no closer than that. Here in connection with the celebrations and opening of the new Town Hall by the then Prince George, 'the latest SR engine and rolling stock' were available for inspection at the station. The loco is a 4-6-0 'Lord Nelson'.

A queue of boys — only one female is present — are waiting to view the ex-works No 34090 *Sir Eustace Missenden — Southern Railway* at an open day, the location and date of which have not been recorded.

Top left: In the event this view was not used, with the comment, 'Story killed' being on the file print. The caption commented, 'Boy Goes to see the King', January 1947. 'Picture Post sent a photographer along to record the actions of a young boy, Michael Hardy, who makes a trip to Buckingham Palace in the hopes of seeing the Royal Family leave for their South African tour'.

Left: Adverse weather conditions on 27 January 1954. Evidently also electrification had been extended to Southampton by that date (!) as the caption read, 'A general view of the heavy snow at Hazlemere (sic) Station as a postman waits on the platform for the London train to come in from Southampton'. If we are to believe the rest of the story, drifts of three feet of snow were lying in the area of the town.

Above: Porter Fred Eeles of Kenley mows the lawn on Platforms 2 and 3 at Coulsdon North station. The station gardens here were reported as having won several prizes.

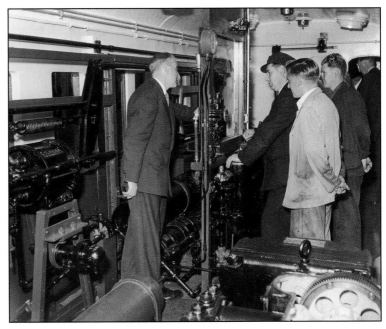

Above: Staff training is a crucial part of railway operation and in the 1950s several former '3SUB' electric units were converted into mobile training schools. The original copy supplied with this print reads: 'Mobile School for Railway Trainees — With the extension of electrification on the Southern Region of British Railways, many more trainees are being recruited for the servicing and maintenance of electric rolling stock and existing staff have to be kept abreast of new techniques and equipment. Therefore the Southern Region have planned and built a three-coach Instructional train, which travels to various depots, avoiding the large amount of travelling which would be required if trainees were required to attend a central instructional school. This train is, in effect a "mobile school", fitted with working specimens of all the various items and types of equipment with which the trainees will have to deal. There is also a lecture room aboard and the number of men in each class is strictly limited, making individual attention possible. A class is seen in progress in the brake chamber of the train at Waterloo. The Instructor is Mr F.T. Littlefield of Chessington (left), with his pupils, Raymond Evans and Peter Stoneman of Waterloo who are watching Norman Cowan of Twickenham at the controls. This particular chamber has working apparatus for instruction on operation and maintenance of automatic and electro-pneumatic brake operation.'

Left: Steam working on the Kent Coast line, represented by 'Schools' class No 30915 *Brighton* passing through an unrecorded location. The notes on the file print record that the estimated cost of the Kent Coast improvements was some £25 million, which included the electrification of 80 miles of track, civil engineering improvements, new signalling and new rolling stock and depot facilities.

Below: The inaugural run of Bulleid's double-deck unit No 4002 on Tuesday 1 November 1949. The unit is seen approaching Waterloo Junction on its run from Charing Cross. After just a short period of running both double-deck sets had to be taken out of service owing to cracks in their wheels. The replacements were of stronger construction rather than just being a scaled down version of the ordinary carriage wheel and no further difficulties were encountered.

Right: Orpington car sheds and washing plant, 21 March 1946. This was one of a number of EMU depots and carriage sheds of similar style which were built with the expansion of the electrified network. This particular depot dated from 1925.

Above: 'Ghost Trains — A product of six years research by Southern Railway technicians, Britain's nationalised railways have a force of nine "ghost" trains specially equipped to fight the frost menace on London and south-eastern tracks. The 'admiralty bronze' shoes of the trains lay on the live rail and distribute a half-inch wide stream of anti-freeze oil or de-icing fluid. Each of the trains has a crew of three, and the oil carriage attached has an operative capacity of 750 gallons. The striking force of anti-freeze trains is planned to prevent a repetition of last winter's great freeze up, and is strategically dispersed from Portsmouth in the east to Hastings in the east. It is controlled from headquarters at London Bridge, where weather reports are received from the admiralty. The view shows an engineer at the knee-hole desk in the oil carriage and which operate at 60mph.''
The photograph is dated 21 January 1948.

Right: The Sydenham Hill end of Penge Tunnel. Due to its length of more than 1¼ miles, repeating distant signals were provided.

Above: Electrification work at New Eltham. A train of 'EPB' stock, with set S5050 trailing, passes, while the gentleman on the right appears to be taking a recklessly cavalier attitude to the dangers posed by an energised third rail.

Right: Extension of the third rail westwards came with the 22-route-mile electrification from Woking through Brookwood to Aldershot, Farnham and Alton. On 5 July 1937 — the first day of the new service — a '4COR' set is seen alongside an 'M7' at Aldershot.

Far right: Although no date is appended to this print, this is believed to be of the inauguration of the Brighton line electrification in the 1930s. The motorman is receiving a ceremonial send off.

Above: One of the new electric trains leaves Dartford Junction on 6 June 1926. The electrification was part of an £8 million investment by the newly-formed Southern Railway in its suburban network.

Left: The new electric service, recorded at Blackheath on 6 June 1926. This was the first day of what was a 'restricted service' using electric traction on the route from Charing Cross and Cannon Street to Dartford, the full service commencing a few weeks later from 19 July.

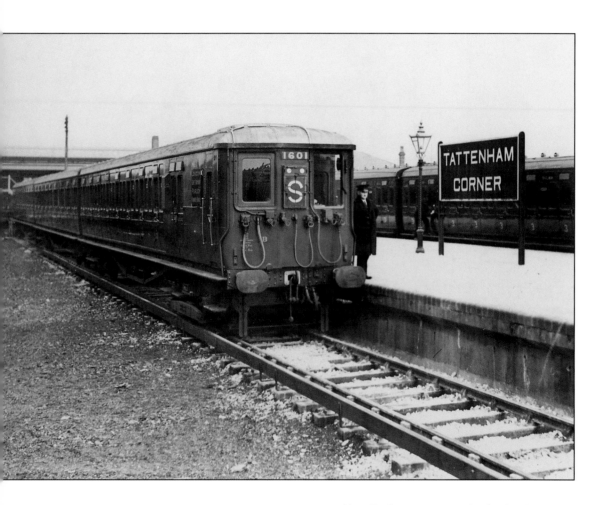

Above: The first passenger carrying electric train arrives at Tattenham Corner in March 1928, formed of '3SUB' set No 1601, which had been converted from SECR steam-hauled stock.

Right: Celebrations at Bognor Regis on 30 June 1938. This was the official inauguration day for electric services on the Bognor branch as well as to Littlehampton and Chichester — public electric service started on 3 July. The new order is represented by newly-built '2BIL' unit No 2104, while in the opposite platform a rake of hauled stock including LBSCR 'balloon' vehicles shows what is about to be swept away.

The Wimbledon flyover was built to separate local and suburban traffic from main line workings, taking away the need for trains to cross over running lines using points on the level, this allowing services to be speeded up and run at a greater frequency. These views of its construction date from February 1936. The 700yd long structure remains in use today.

With car 8465 leading, three-car '3SUB' No 1520 of 1925 brings a service into Waterloo in March 1938 The letter 'S' signified a train from Shepperton via Kingston and New Malden.

Above: Further examples of Bulleid's innovation were the three main line diesel-electric locomotives Nos 10201-3, which he masterminded. Although rated at only 1,600hp, and thus small by modern standards, Nos 10201 and 10202, along with the more powerful 10203, displayed a degree of operational flexibility which surprised many. With its body and bogie design prepared at Ashford Works and using an English Electric power plant, No 10202 is seen at Waterloo on 15 October 1951. The locomotives remained on the Southern Region until 1955, after which they worked out the rest of their existence on the London Midland Region.

Left: Level crossing at Twickenham. Wooden gates were considered of sufficient strength to stop a road vehicle running at moderate speed.

Above: The Southern Railway's last Chief Mechanical Engineer, O. V. S. Bulleid, was noted for introducing revolutionary new ideas. Alongside his Pacifics with their oil bath chain drives and his double-deck units, one of his most heterodox innovations was the 'Tavern car'. These were buffet and restaurant cars in the style of public houses, with mock brickwork painted on their exteriors and ersatz timber beams inside, as seen here.

Left: All the Tavern cars had 'pub names' — this is the *Jolly Tar* being inspected by passengers at Waterloo on 25 May 1949. The man does not appear to be too impressed, although the ladies might take a different perspective.

Right: Vandalism became an pressing problem during the 1960s and early 1970s and continued to increase as platform staff were reduced. Here in January 1970, Station Master Mr W. H. Brown inspects the damage to an electric multiple-unit at set at New Cross after its use on a soccer special for Tottenham Hotspur fans. Tottenham was knocked out of the FA Cup at Crystal Palace and fans went on the rampage. Windows in the booking office and parcels office at Norwood Junction were smashed, while the football special only managed to travel a short distance before having to be taken out of service due to broken windows, ripped seats, broken light bulbs and the communication cord being pulled several times.

A bold attempt was made in the 1960s to revive rural railways by the retired wing commander Mr Ashby Sadler. Mr Sadler leased the truncated remains of the Meon Valley line at Droxford for experiments with his Pacerailer rail bus. He intended that the rail bus would be used on the soon-to-be closed Isle of Wight lines. Unfortunately, as with similar experiments in the past savings would be limited as the existing rails and infrastructure would still be needed. The Sadler vehicle did make a demonstration trip to the Island, where it appears to have been regarded more as a gimmick than a serious attempt at a railway revival. It was said to be fitted with air conditioning and ran on rubber pneumatic tyres. Having failed to secure a future for his invention Mr Sadler's vehicle was destroyed by fire at Droxford under circumstances which have still not been explained.

Left: In the interim stage between closure and dismantling, sections of what is today the Bluebell Railway were used for the storage of condemned wagons. This was the scene at Kingscote, north of Hosted Keynes, on 12 March 1959, looking towards East Grinstead.. The platform canopy supports have evidently not been repainted since World War 2.

Below: The new station at Southampton West (later to be renamed Southampton Central) under construction in May 1935. The Southern was an enthusiastic user of concrete and the development of the station was referred to in the caption details as part of the SR's investment in the expansion of Southampton Docks.

Left: Work is being undertaken on an electricity substation near Lewes on 21 November 1934, as part of the expansion of the third rail network to Eastbourne. There were many such substations on the electrified lines of the Southern.

Below: Electrification in the BR era. The Kent Coast scheme of the late 1950s involved the widening of sections of the railway and new platforms were required. Here at St Mary Cray a new island platform is being built. The works were photographed on 19 March 1959.

The Kent Coast electrification required widening of the line at Bickley. On 19 March 1959, the train headed by the now-preserved No 34027 *Taw Valley* is working between Charing Cross and Folkestone/Dover, while underneath work is underway widening the Margate and Ramsgate line.

Above: The remains of Cannon Street signalbox after it was destroyed by fire in the early hours of 5 April 1957. Understandably, no trains were running that morning, although a limited service was in operation very shortly afterwards.

Left: A Class C 0-6-0 travels light engine across the widened bridges near St Mary Cray on 19 March 1959.

Below: The official opening of the Freight Transport Exhibition at Battersea Wharf on 30 October 1958. A container is seen being lifted on to a Conflat wagon. Today, the containers, cranes and road vehicles are larger, but the same principles are used.

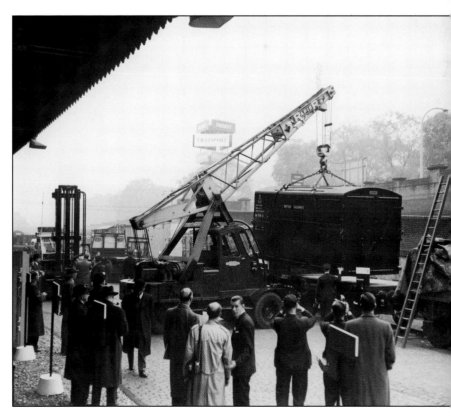

Above: Victoria in August 1936, with huge crowds waiting to board trains. Even at this time , the electric services of the Southern Railway were operated in fixed formations, although there were sets of excursion carriage which could be pressed into use at busy times like this.

Right: The Western side of Victoria, photographed on 11 February 1939. The Eastern and Western side of Victoria appeared to virtually be two separate stations until the 1990s when concourse work including a new W. H. Smiths store broke down the wall between the two. The photographer's notes record that the platforms here were a quarter of a mile long. They are a little shorter today as the station concourse has been extended over some of the track area. In the 1980s the Victoria Place shopping centre was built above these platforms, maximising BR's assets at this central London location.

Left: Victoria station, and the advance guard of holiday makers off on a tour of Italy, 24 March 1937. The caption reported they would use the same train throughout the whole of the 15 day trip — does this mean the carriages were literally shipped across as well? Buttonholes are being presented to passengers just prior to departure.

Above: Bridge collapse at Aspinal Road, Brockley, on 29 November 1960. Luckily the collapse occurred during the night and casualties were avoided. There was, however, considerable disruption to services on the Dartford Loop and Bexleyheath lines to Blackfriars and Holborn the following day.

The aftermath of the Eastbourne accident of 25 August
1958. Six passengers were killed when a steam-hauled train
from Glasgow crashed into an electric service from Ore to
London Bridge, which was just about the leave the station.
The crew of the steam-hauled excursion were found to
have run past a stop signal set to danger, and the collision
occurred at a speed of 25mph.